Reality Checkmate

Reality Checkmate

Daniel Ruiz

Four Way Books
Tribeca

for Mayoya, Pops, and Ale

Library of Congress Cataloging-in-Publication Data

Names: Ruiz, Daniel (Poet), author.
Title: Reality checkmate / Daniel Ruiz.
Description: New York : Four Way Books, 2025.
Identifiers: LCCN 2024037092 (print) | LCCN 2024037093 (ebook) | ISBN
9781961897380 (trade paperback) | ISBN 9781961897397 (ebook)
Subjects: LCGFT: Poetry.
Classification: LCC PS3618.U535 R43 2025 (print) | LCC PS3618.U535
(ebook) | DDC 811/.6--dc23/eng/20240828
LC record available at https://lccn.loc.gov/2024037092
LC ebook record available at https://lccn.loc.gov/2024037093

This book is manufactured in the United States of America and printed on
acid-free paper.

Four Way Books is a not-for-profit literary press. We are grateful for the assistance
we receive from individual donors, public arts agencies, and private foundations
including the NEA, and the New York State Council on the Arts, a state agency.

We are a proud member of the Community of Literary Magazines and Presses.

Contents

The fire is coming.
It says to wait.
—John Ashbery

Valor

No one wants to be rescued.
To be the hero of the story,
to call it a story at all, so that it merits a hero,
a situation no one wants is saved from turning into

what nightmares dream of. The nightmare is staved off,
so we blame the hero, half having wanted to see
what evil could come up with—a bird beak on a human face,
guns for arms, spiked skin—but that's all right.

We settle for thinking it up, so the hero can live
in celebrity far beyond the utility of their story,
about which we need constant reminders.

The sounds of explosions can be explained
away. No missile retires early
growing up on hero stories.

Drum Solo

After Nicanor Parra

Since what has happened is bound to renew itself
with the variety and viciousness of funhouse mirrors
when you are already drunk and desperate to escape;

since the landscape is landlocked; since we imagine
ourselves with wings but not that birds might want
another life, as we want another life, and the beat

wants to repeat itself ad infinitum, giving up
on finding a center, as if in the ocean somewhere
a giant seashell, weakened by water, wanted

not to chip away in fragments later found at the beach
but to revel in its unity, as one does in their sleep,
aimless and alert as the great teachings of sidewalks

and skyscrapers, kiosks and coffees and vape pens
wear off; since it all wears off and slides down
the hair on your body until it coalesces

with the world, you cannot be part of it, distant
as your two arms yet near as the Department of Images
to the eye, behind a short door intruders don't see;

since I see it, and walk through abandoned rooms
my other lives might have happened in, and the story
finds itself disliking the telling, disagreeing with

the sad tone of late; I want to start over
without repeating, even if it costs me
another life.

Beware of God

Under the falling coffering,
all sounds stand still.

The dome prepares
a presentation of wreckage
for the floral floor mural.

Now sunbeams marinate shards
that hang in the palace
like meteoric chandeliers.

      ***

There's nothing like watching
the airplane's wings wobble,

no replacement for feeling
like an arrow shot
through a hall of mirrors,

nothing to be done
about the storm above the stage.

Above it, a hand sprinkles
lightning bolts. Above that hand
another stage.

***

You who scrub
white the iris, who breathe
on windows only to write,
beware the boiling water,
your face among the bubbles.

In the woods of monotony,
the immortals aren't anti-
life. They are hiding
behind the double
double doors.

Complicit in the Clangor

Stuck in the sky's mind, desire seeks
a new cloud to chase down what flies out,
but following the mountain path,
when one of us slides on sediment,

it's an avalanche for fire ants,
a rocket launch in our windpipes.
The escalator back to that vista
we went so far out of our way to witness

knocks the ceiling of our skulls
like water against a geyser's cork.
So much novelty burns to fizzle out.
So many stones rubbed together

while, nearby, an inferno waits
with a glass of water. Whole empires
are built on this principle. Someone submerged
in a poison puddle emerges a Venus flytrap.

Lorca says a caterpillar roams the mind
devouring philosophers, but in a caterpillar's mind
philosophers operate on butterflies. The red arrow
on the map points to a castle and says

YOU ARE NOT HERE.

Whole principles are built on this empire.

Is this your card, a smile on a skull?

Is this your skull, a lantern on a spear?

Reincarnation

Riptide aches the moon's
ankles. Mahi massage them
into a whirlpool
out of which a shipwreck rises.

On tiptoe, I see you
on tiptoe,

balancing on the snapped mast
like a tightrope walker.
Now, from the shore,
like a tightrope walker
balancing on a snapped mast

on tiptoe, on tiptoe
I see you

writhing over the shipwreck's
whirlpool, reading the message
written in upturned Mahi: don't
make me repeat myself

Master of Fine Arts

to Vicente Huidobro

God is an exiled carpenter
from an even grander universe
where He first had to be raised,
educated, and socialized before
they gave Him a reality to govern
and this is the one He got stuck with.

We're in the same position, which isn't
what He expected. I mean, what's so great
about God, God, God? I translate Lorca
and he says, "Love, love, love,"
and now I'm suspicious of statues.

What's so beautiful about a monument
are the centuries of bystanders
reading the dedicative plaque and at once
feeling lifted to historical significance
and like the gorgeous, memorized
names of the famously dead
have been demystified. They're there,

beside us, desperate for a bathroom
and some nourishment and a society
that likes their ideas more than the one
that killed them. And God
knows all about that, being a minor poet
Himself, even in His homeland, where He's riled up
in eternal quarantine from the beings He's commanded
to love Him, or else.

                            Vicente, our God is not
an elegant condor marinating on a branch
but the dynasty of pigeons who, because
they don't mind walking, deny us the chance
to toss our crumbs at the sky.

Sunrise and Shadow

I can see good things from the horizon:
how blocky buildings are; how blocky
fields of undistinguished fields, or skyscrapers
in gardens of skyscrapers, are; how small
my friends look, waving at me on my upward cloud.

It's all I ever wanted at a distance I do not like.
The problem with visions of the world as snowglobe
is floating, the problem with floating is falling,
and the problem with falling is the snowglobe
never stops shaking, making winter eternal

for its inhabitants, who, though imaginary,
have form, are physical. What's imagined
is their motion into and out of small houses
oblivious to gravity, but the premium on motion,
the culture of motion so toxic, sleep is the space

for the made-up, the mattress the launchpad
where dream is diluted to anecdote and analysis
lifted to imagery, can hardly be called imaginary.
It's a second self a tolerance can be built towards
with no effort, a side effect of surviving minus

the wash of fields, the wobble of skyscrapers,
not seeing all the small talk we practiced for hours
in the mirror, to make the business of living easier
when the business day ended, put to good use.
We all have one, and fear it might usurp us,

following the foggy logic of seasons
running into one another until some day
deep into the next one, the sweater
or the swimsuit draped over the desk chair
no longer applies. The horizon no longer applies.

Methinks

Therefore androids be programmed to believe
in reincarnation, press their own off-buttons, possess the self-
discipline of a poster to settle for semblance. Why do people name
cars but not houses? To pretend they move. To absolve themselves
of the perceived smile bisecting a bumper, headlights a euphemism,
the opposite of eyes, two sunspots stuffed into plastic cockpits
below a crystal forehead some bug has been smeared across.
Now a friend comes to visit. Now the coffee I killed this morning
with a massive swig, to live again, must leave me like alert
ants fleeing the jeans they crawled onto ten mornings ago, hoping
the land was full of spices, disappointed by a denim sea and pasta
fossils. I don't trust my judgment. I can barely separate my clothes
into piles—*keep, donate, destroy*—and sometimes it's human enough
to wonder whether everyone you know also grabs their stomach fat
to talk with their bellybutton; or walks down whole boulevards
resisting an itch over a clump of fabric; whether they spread-eagle
over their mattress after a long day like a hand on top
of all the strawberries at a friend's birthday party; or not.

Stitches After Reading Márquez

The skin is open
and it hurts even more
to sew it back together

and when the snakes
return to Macondo
they all say *You'll be fine*

which I almost
believe because if animals
are talking

who knows
what else is happening
who knows

how many volcanoes
woke up today
and did not erupt

how many storms
parked their clouds
over the world

and said
I'm too tired
who knows

about the children
born with the tails of pigs
or horns

that break the skin
when you pet their heads
I've spent all summer

digging toward
the metal heart of mangos
with my teeth

growing snakes
in my yard and consulting
the Oracle on which color

to paint my house
I've taken birds
from wooden barstools

and set them free
in my apartment
I've left my door

unlocked but closed
because who's
going to try me

who's ready
to barge in and steal
my frozen bananas

and take my pictures
from their frames
and nap on my couch

before cutting me
open for the surgery
of a lifetime

where my skin
is polished into glass
and I'm knocked

off the counter
and shatter
before I hit

the wooden floor

Nerve Endings

Is it cruel, the mirror
in the birdcage, the wings
painted on downtown's brick walls?
Can you repeat the question?

So that I cannot be snuck up on.
So that I know what it's in response to.
Though I did all I could to avoid it,
this answered an era of stasis,

which doesn't mean it ended. Answer
me—what does it say about god
that his most common imitator
is a dictator, not an artist? Answer me.

Panorama in Night Vision

There are easier ways to die happy.
One day a baseball zips through a store aisle
begging for contact. The next, your lost love finds you
dehydrated in the food court. Isolated,
these incidents teach us the wrong lesson, leaving
only the impulse to keep scouring the junkyard
for artifacts among the mold and viscera
of old food and metals, but through fusion
you begin to comprehend the use of chance,
like a many-sided die. You feel like someone pleasure reading
in front of a live studio audience, and even more so when it airs
and you're there to see how stern your eyebrows and forehead
look, as if you were trying to read the backside of the page.

It says, "If you can read this sign, I can't see you"—
you, the novelist whose protagonist shares your name,
asserting your non-existence; you, sneaky as the *p* in raspberry,
building statues of avalanches for a figure drawing class;
or you, blasting Schubert in the Whataburger drive-thru,
condescending to your sandwich. You are a composite
of shit, memory, and nightmare, and the lines between them,
within yourself, blur like lightning when you blink.

If the mirror were see-through, the empire of invisibility
could train your shadow to be a ghost. Instead,
the road explodes into an octopus of paths,
a lone flame sparked in the center, and you don't know
which to take. Your magic trick?
Inventing a new magic trick. Pain gurgles back up
the garbage disposal, helplessly whining, "Water,"
encouraging indulgence in confusing image systems
meant to make you think about yourself
when you've done nothing wrong. The whole time
you thought you were nerfed by verdict, allergic to insight,
that central flame was busy making fire angels of the grass.

Of course you want the landscape to glimmer,
but you can't ignore the thousands
of dried-up seeds and scorched roots, and farther out still
some frozen in ice so dense no light could penetrate it enough
to splash them awake. Move out from behind the camera.
Use your hand to block the sun. You'll see
the trenches in ruin from pole to pole
and only the occasional flashbang from beneath the dirt,
giving you occasion to feel effulgent against the field
but wishing it were greener still—*full of fucking flowers!*
you can't believe you think to yourself, you derivate scoundrel!

yet you are here, examining the meadows of dirt, trying to
think of a new word for green.

Like I said, there are easier ways to die happy.
You could squint through the spyglass backwards like a straw
and roll the map peeled off the globe onto the table,
trying to flatten out the sides in denial of the warped world.
Does it look ugly to you, in your head, where you can privately
explore the extremes?

Madrugada

The soft trumpet waking me up
belongs to Miles Davis. The lamp's beams
on my eyes are connected to a head world
famous for headaches. My work
confuses me. What's so special about breaking longer lines
into shorter lines
is something I never could articulate beyond
the sensation that language, set down
on a page, actually furiously moves
omnidirectionally, as wind
rubs water to form waves which travel
800 km/hr to lick
the shoreline into shape, a giraffe's tongue
on a tourist's head. There's a difference
between a year of dying and a year of the dead,
checkbooks and checkpoints, logic and rope.
The sword's blade sharpens as you trace it
downward, leaving a cut that shoots up.
Many things made of steel
wobble in the wind, existing not
on the page. Some days I wake
and worship the dead. Others
I snap off the mattress,
throw myself onto the porch,

and argue with the grackles
over whom my neighbor's illegal roosters
prefer to hear sing. That's just the side
of the sun I'm on. You for whom meaning
is the meaning of beauty, be gone.
You clap too loud
to hear the rooster's response. Meanwhile,
the clouds are proud of all of us. It's 12:01.
A man dragged by a poodle says
Good morning. Everyone in the orchestra
stands up at once.

Some Verses

There's the universe, the multiverse, and the philosophers they try to hide from;
the zigzags of grandparents' marriages, mirages of grandfather clocks;
then there's the rising stock, the livestock, the market both super and not.

An old couple lifts a watermelon then drops it in their shopping cart.
When later they take turns holding and slicing it, before turning on the TV,
the perfection of their form brings the questioning of forms into question,

reversing our launch instead toward those midnight lights
in the marketplace where people who have nowhere to go can
safely bite the loudest apples.

The History of Entertainment

Might as well call it
>   the history of attention, of attention
spans. Might as well stand
>   on the corner and sing

to see where that gets you,
>   analyze the effectiveness of drum
solos. Might as well be the lamp
>   who did it, all this lounging

in the passive voice, the words
>   nowhere and nothing rushing
out of abstraction to mean a field
>   that is all snow or meadow,

unclumped by hills; meanwhile
>   what makes it so makes it so
fucking boring you can't sell it.
>   Might as well admit the shock

was more valuable than anticipated,
>   considering how impossible it is
not to look at lightning
>   lighting a river up

when all we wanted was
            to float. Might as well
walk the walk backwards
            to empathize with the eye

as it's forced to keep
            staring into an advancing
burning horizon, but I'm not sure
            I agree with that.

Your dreams are burning
            in a mansion in the slush
with all the other applicants, and that
            invisibility is verified.

Besides, it's so easy
            to make a nightmare,
you do it ten times an hour
            without trying. Try trying.

Peripheral Explosions

There's no Icarus without sea, sky, trumpets,
no remorse in the painted ricochet of realities and rockets.

When the plane lands and becomes a car
and the spoon catapults an egg, the eye
prefers to close, repulsed by light
like a bedroom. A skeleton
uses its spine as a walking stick
to hitchhike across the country
and dig up its one true love.

Without a story, it's still a story.
Time passes, you're reading, that's the story,
and an image has no need to narrate.
It lives in your eye, under an assembly line of perceptions.
In the Detention Center, badged guards roam,
praying to the portrait of your desperation,
which seems so natural to them, it becomes an exhibit
your entire existence gets stored beneath.

O ghost in a large white sheet, eye sockets scissored open—
behind every firing squad, a photographer; the Antichrist calling Christ
the Antichrist; the body the only bystander—

but not in this realm.
I used to be a sack of cells,
now I'm the Architect of Water.

Argument with an Elevator

A couch inches
off a truck bed
into traffic.

An old guy says
the city was better
in the eighties.

A puppy pulls
a pant leg
down an ankle

and you mitigate
ache by freezing
your ligaments solid.

Stop. Do not be so ill-
paired as the highway
and the golf course.

When I asked my dad
if he liked pineapple
on pizza, he held a globe

up to my face and said,
"There's a reason Italy
and Hawaii are so far apart,

mijo." He was talking about
plate tectonics, the Grand
Canyon's grandpa.

He thinks if we could only
vacuum up the water
filling the core's craters,

the years would jumble
their numbers as the sand
into which they're inscribed

sloshes like the ashes
in the cathedral
of a falling urn.

Suspended: call it
sky. Shattered:
a blender.

There's only so much nuance
can do before you realize
you're trapped in a mind

you don't like, pulling
out electrical wires, confused
by the back of the eye

when the best virtual
reality helmet there is
is a blindfold.

Inferno Use Only

See the serpents slinking towards you? Their fangs
don't know their future as trinkets, the friction between
the A- and B-sides of bisected empires, the requisite recklessness

colored over like the many faces of a mural. They slither
around and beyond you as if you were a boulder
on a bike trail, leaving the strange wish to be bitten

while the rhythm you roamed to in search
of that venomous antidote is awkward now, mere math.
You spear onward through the frozen marshes

where black ice becomes a ballroom for mud
but, like a page torn off a desktop calendar,
every day you're flung one backwards.

It's the part they don't print in the manual:
once admitted to your new reality,
you have to kill the you who's there.

Otherwise, you're not yourself out there: the rocks
you hurl ping back into the reservoir, lost
in the fogged-up horizon, and you begin to scrutinize

the seams of your reflection because something
assimilates into a purgatory of distances. As Milton says,
"The great hierarchical standard was to move."

There's a genre of epiphany called
genre epiphany. It lights the brain's
hollow emeralds, makes strangers smile

at each other's stares. It glows but it's empty
inside the lightbulb, too hot to touch the horse's hair.
You cannot rearrange the mountains from least to greatest.

You can only wish for sympathy when the lampshade rips
above you as the boy king straightens
his concomitant five-turreted mural crown.

Double Bacon

At the cocktail party, it was hard to tell
        who you meant to talk about. We'd been speaking
double all night long, attuned to the coast of humor
        just beyond oceanic monologues, all of us
taking turns demonstrating our evening attire—
        capes, gowns, heels, crowns—all prepared
to respond courteously to any etiquetical slide in the mud.

So when you began to describe England's High Chancellor
        as a painter "descendant of Raphael" and the portraitist
who had "familial connections which eased his way up
        the political ladder," the mixed images of these men
opened a wrinkle on an unmade bed in my mind,
        where I found a remote control. I began to mash its buttons.
Every light in the mansion blinked on and off on repeat.
        Under the blanket over the table were aluminum bowls
of white feathers. Red halos glowed on the floor around every heel.

You could say I was daydreaming, I guess,
        but out of everyone balancing little plates of deviled eggs,
I think I followed your point most faithfully.
        After all, these two shared more than just a name, right?
The statesman fathered the scientific method and empiricism,
        which still work in almost all scenarios. The painter did figurative work

instead of forgetting the body, which is where these theories are,

    at cocktail parties, tested. They could've attempted a friendship right here.

It's not like either one of them wouldn't've been invited.

Las Meninas

It's hard not to feel seen by Velazquez

but like a portrait in a courtroom
the lines eyes make can be interpreted

around the room, in this painting
of ourselves no one sees

save Velazquez, a painter with many statues
in Spain, whose eyes

move not.

Reality Checkmate

I thought we were all harkening
back to tell Don Quixote
Foucault said he invented

humans, and now all of us are
eternally punished with proving
literature is about literature

after all—after all
those years of not even
needing to write it down,

then writing it to praise
someone with way more
power than you, then

writing about a flower
to piss off someone
with way more power than you,

who feels entitled to praise.
I guess I was wrong
about the battleships

we boasted atop: a shepherd
makes a great captain
because his sailors know

they won't survive the sea.
Meanwhile, a lost sheep
finds grass to eat

anywhere it wants,
and does not mind,
like Lorca, letting its hair

grow long. This sea
we worship is for worship
only. In it float sheep.

What about me?

Too Much Interpretation

My days of hanging out in front of the gas station
are over. Now I'm a poet, trash is glorious.
Riding the escalator as it floats over
the mall's forty-foot Christmas tree
is glorious. Ankle weights, soreness
of the ankles pulsing while elevated
above a pillow is glorious. Now I'm a poet
who's looking for a line-sized question
to juxtapose all the imagery I had planned.
My house is bigger on the inside. The shadows
seated on my couch's shadow
belong to me.

Embodied Cognition

It's just like writing poems. You think
you're driving the car
but you're the coffee spill on the steering wheel,
the door slammed on a fingernail,

the receiver, not the transmitter,
who embodies the posture of freedom. *Questions?*
Always. We are one big personality test.
Do dice or boxing gloves hang from your rearview mirror?
Which side of the bed do you sleep on—above or below?

It all boils down to your own vulnerability.
People singing in other cars look like they bite the air.
I have heard many rich people say, "There is a natural
order to this world, which is in the shape of a box of toys.
You put the ones you play with on top of all the others,"

but I am unconvinced. I am driven into a tunnel
and forced to slow down. Suddenly it jams with singers
who mock the exhaust smoking up the windshields,
whose windpipes enjoy the cryogenesis of A/C.
There is no other way to be invulnerable.
If we are the product of a pang, we are created

in a mouth
by some singer biting the air.

Remnants of Empire

The equestrian statues of kings
from various plazas I've seen
come together in the plaza
of the mind, crowding a small garden
with Charles's, and Edwards's—
the stench of piss ringed around
each base making logical the many
footprints denoting a darkness
of soil between strokes of green.

This impulse has to be questioned.
A country is made up of people
as an ocean is a mausoleum
of raindrops dying for unity,
as the sun's embers yearn
to be distinguished as flares.
Why else put a statue up there,
if not to say, in this land,
these are the statues? Why not
make them larger than life to imply
History's bigness, and dominance?

You wake to it every day.
Landscape of Sun with Burning Horses.

Landscape of Landscapes Superimposed—
bad idea. All the world aches. The aches
accumulate into something greater. The horses
carry something heavier than kings—metal,
which is why they ordered their legs
so thin, their bases so heavy,
they cannot run.

Wrong Answers Only

I miss the world of old words:
apoplexy, ataraxy, back when
E Pluribus Unum meant something.

But I love the world of new words,
where everything has come a ways
away from the mountains and factories

where caoutchouc is vulcanized to rubber.
Everything else? Derivative of daffodils.
Doused in decoration, nothing

cares to soar. Double doors open
on a courtyard chockablock with blossoms
contained by a chainlink fence. The president,

like a wind-up sailboat released
in a bubble bath, crosses the central path,
leafing through stacks of documents

his conversations can't keep up with. "The Allegory
of the Cave," applied to the mind, still leaves one
seeking alternative exit strategies. No one

trusts the attention span of the eye
to keep its flamethrowers forever
aimed forward. Industry creeps

out the metaphoric. Something else
has been given the job of expanding
the cave in place of words. Someone else

has unloaded a topography of furniture
to minimize the echo, O receipt
of the real. But this leads to all

genres of confusion. A continent away,
a landscape painter hides in the trenches,
memorizing the confetti of crossfire.

Coming Soon

You get to be a star
yet you wanted to be a comet.
You are a landscape painter
in a steel city, briefcase
plump with brushes;

a Wall Street banker already
sweaty from a backpack
of workout clothes.
A skyscraper casts
an enormous shadow

neither God nor God Particle
can explain or lift
off the sidewalk, but when
captured in a triptych
or questioned in a public square,

the forms of what are and are not
boycott our examination
there, where the final
row of unmasked mobsters
scatters one-by-one

from the riot amassing
momentum, the slow-motion
explosions soon to be superimposed
by classical music in the movie
version of our lives.

You get to be a mind
watching the towers crumble
yet you wanted to be a body
breaking, breaking
for cover beyond the blast radius

as Ozymandias erupts from eternal sand.

Creation Myth

Day is on inside out.
     The moon's in flames,
man lands on the sun,
     and at night roosters
caw us to sleep. Even
     you wake up before me
now, turning off my alarm
     before my mind snaps
out of my dream of me
     sleeping. But I am always
awake, my eyes are just closed.
     Just last night I watched you
as the sun rose to pour darkness
     in our window, to smother
you in it as you pulled the curtain,
     which only spotlighted
the keyhole of your shadow
     shining behind your back.

Or Else No More Pleasure

After the movie, the pleasant
tone, induced by music, persists,
and the streets seem suddenly safer.
Lovers walk them now, newly
oblivious to the wind their faces

confront, confident having overcome
all that plot—all to return to the room
unrecognizable to one another,
the way trees look at seeds. Split
by loneliness their love disintegrates

like a falling building. And the streets,
walking them home after, seem only
full of names. It makes one wonder
what the value of likeness is
and is like. Exaggeration is for argument

only, which is why music is always
persuasive; which is why, leaving
the theater now, my friend,
we're the lovers, precisely because
we're not. Every year there's a winter

the wind takes no responsibility for,
a landscape chafed by gust, we live
to feel as images do, adjective-worthy,
visible as hundreds of highway trees
in which hundreds of birds are invisible.

Nothing, my friend, makes us
hunger more than our own image
adjective-less; nothing escapes us
quicker than when our mouths are open.
Our ghosts report back to their bodies,
where they feel colossal, and safe.

Agenda

All that's left is to be happy.
We've tried letting closing doors
crunch our fingers, reaching
for a bite of white bread; seen
every episode of this season's
war on a cheap television set;
sat at bus stops mid-flood,
hoping. We have fought back
but forgotten, or tried to forget
the tide of bones the sand sits on
as high tide eats the shore.
You've got to stare at a mountain
for centuries to notice it move
an inch. If the moon crumbled,
we'd be the pinball that broke the glass.
But, now, the only thing is to be happy.
We have tried everything else.

Reading *The Cantos* in the Bathtub

I feel like a true poet today after guessing
the grapefruit's faces at the grocery store with Shangyang

Now I lie neck-deep in a bubble bath
reading so close to where so many poets believe this book belongs

I don't pretend to understand it I don't even understand Shangyang
and we just spent two hours plucking bald a pineapple we didn't even buy

The shampoo watches my knees bend and extend confused
because they look like mountains sprouting out of the ocean

like a revived rocketship's hard-on for the reappearing moon
O moon Jane says you're too close to the sun right now

but survive its orbit of ember and you'll return
to your horizon more alive and more flustered

than a sailor who harpoons into a supermarket of waves
and resurfaces holding the eraserless pencil he dropped off his rowboat

I Took a Hammer to My Tomb

Shut up. There will come a day when I no longer know you,
when I say, "I vaguely remember someone
with that name," and wince like my cheek and forehead
are trying to shut my eyes for me. Mother!
Tell me the home movies aren't all lost. Tell me
my experience has been continuous since birth.
Some days I sit and stare at my hands and forget
they touched a Monet when the guard
with his hands in his pockets ambled
to the next room. Can you believe I used to imagine
you naked in the kitchen, picking an apple
from the bowl, washing it in our sink, and putting it back?
But I don't know what your body looks like anymore.
I don't know where your legs stop or the height
of your mouth against my chest. In a silent room,
even a pen clicking is loud. We have left the TV on
again for the room to watch, and now my heartbeat is fat
from too much coffee. Do you remember how
I worshipped you? You who season your chicken
with water. You who write your checks in pencil.
Remember that God, too, is an individual
I used to worship. He has His opinions.
So do you, so do I. Now, when I see you again
you are ugly, and haven't changed at all. I'm happy.

I'm watching movies in my underwear, and my hammer,
covered in the dust of smashed concrete, reclines
on the table and would stand were it lighter, and when
I grab the wooden handle to pick it up, I know I'm shaking
bigger hands than mine, I know I can carry it
back to the shed, but I don't, and I won't
until I can listen to every song that ever made me cry
without crying; until I can walk in
on the best part of a movie and feel nothing at all.

Babylon

When the white glove strips
the eyebrows from my forehead,
the emeralds from the gutters
between my teeth, then

      then we can leave the party
and explore the stupid streets
of closed banks and black light
bulbs. The river bisects the city

like a tongue gliding over grout.
The windows are open to let
the smoke in. I choose to breathe it,
no better than a tree watching its offering of oxygen
                ignite the houses it serves.

    ii

Ripen, ripen like a sun-seared ruby.

The ground groans as it stretches,
each atom of dirt competing to gain weight.

There, there,
        where even the bricks are asked
for papers, where the packed bus
shatters the communal shroud,
        leaving you behind,

                        there, there,
the clock is black with hands.

        iii

Nowhere are we not chased,
not grabbed after by ghosts
like the Golem feeling the full
weight of its clay limbs.

Death doesn't hear his own rattle
as he stumbles from casket to crime scene,
car crash to cathedral—

can't feel his cloak drag
the big and small clock hands
trying to pin him down like a tent—

and if you think
for one second that the seashells
cemented into balconies love the salt
of foot soles more than they miss
being pushed by impassible waves,
Death is learning to mouth your name.

Loud Laughter

It wafts out of the same demented hallway monsters march out of also:

the vampire sings, laughter follows. A machine modified to present

clear and present danger keeps the bellies stretching silk shirts

bouncing. It is casual Friday on Monday and everyone wants their share

of the orchestra. The ground shakes; it was the earth's laughter forgetting

the whole town sleeps at night. All rise, the chandelier rises by falling

and laughter follows home the man whose car was totaled

on the highway in a hit-and-run. The clerk at the tow yard

laughs at the consistency of accidents, stories of accidents, accidents

caused by looking at accidents. Beneath that junkyard of smashed cars,

the broken jaws of bumpers, there's an underground skyscraper

at the bottom of which someone feels like king. There are no kings only magicians of the singular, making unlike the like.

Bound in image, away they walk.

Still Life at Warp Speed

It's not that I'm not laughing.
      I am. At nothing. I'm trying
to participate in eternity.
      The void appears stretched out
like smoke or a pulled apart mouth,
      the present like a browned toothbrush
you're waiting to get paid again
      to replace. It's gold-rimmed, full
of old water. It's the lost
      head of the vacuum, that slinky
neck, the body plugged in
      somewhere, whirring.

     *

A man with a calf
      tattoo of a bicycle
limps across the crosswalk
      while every bird bobs
its head to the song
      stuck in it. Imagine
the ruckus: all our thoughts
      out loud. That's why
we cover the well.
      You tell a toad

it's croaking, it says,

      "I'm working on my oms."

    *

One by one, lightning

      maims trees, snapping trunks.
All those broken windows.

      All your foes giggling around
a round table. All your clothes

      sucked into the leafblower
as the interviewer calls

      your name. You saw it coming.
Hell, you volunteered.

Archery in an Avalanche

Sometimes I look in the mirror and think
what if I lose myself right now? Like a shark
who, swimming in an ocean of oil,
sees its reflection for the first time.

Then I think it must be different: to invade
a territory around which I've employed
maximum security—yoga,
morning steak or spinach, art therapy—

I must make more than my grand entrance:
I must sneak in, trespass, slip behind my busy eyes.

Again Against Reason

The road leads to more road.

The snake's stomach is another snake.

The movie was based on a true story

Inspired by an old movie

Inspired by a nightmare

Someone woke up

Laughing to. It helped

With the pain. The pain

Helped with the illusion

Of happiness the previous

Owner left in an invisible coat,

Emblazoned with a visible name.

That's how sad they were

Working to be seen, fatigued

From being the shadow's cool,

And not the shadow, shallow-

Minded as mint leaves which only

Taste themselves when ground

With sugar, lifted with rum.

That isn't the world that lies

Like a trunk snapped into someone's yard

But the saunter through sunlight making

The kitchen an oculus, the wails of whale calves

Drowned by orcas muted on a flat

Screen TV. The road leads to more road

Which leads to more

Music, someone else's, and rest stop sex

In the family bathroom after

Hours of driving. Hours of driving

Without yet arriving at the beach

Slathered in red tide. The sand's

Stench rises, mixing with the onslaught of waves

Carrying rotting capelins

The length of the world, of the sea

Which leads to more

Sea, then a shore, the sundry sands

Atop of which the world's waters drum.

Up the Depths

The market is alive with one thousand toothpicks stabbed into olives soaking in white wine. A giant cardboard box only moveable by machine is overwhelmed with watermelons. Now clouds and stars are more than nuts and bolts securing the walls of the sky, provided by the eye that watches like an ostrich in an eggshell, awaiting revolution. Revolution marches out of the mind rewinding. It knows history as the long waterslide you wait in line to ride which ends where the hundred-headed hydra hoards several severed heads in its golden catacomb.

Nitpicking the Gods

After hours in the kitchen,
the unclean oil begs to be scraped
off the pan. The crash test dummy

flung from a model car's windshield
can't stop laughing
just because.

Because is the question
the gods never loved. Because,
like the engine

in the chest of a dove,
the river runs
counter to the plans of the sun.

One cloud cuts off another.
Hence, squalor. Rain, sun, thunder
just because.

Asymptote

Sound of door opening.

Sound of door closing.

Sound of ominous organ music indicating trouble ahead.

Enter Shaman.

Enter man who makes

Sound of thunder by wobbling mirror.

Enter woman who makes

Sound of gunshots by popping balloons.

Curtain. (A field of absence.)

But the play continues:

the male and female leads

return to their dressing rooms

to wipe disinfectant on their lips.

The last three months they've spent

pretending to like each other

but quit? They cannot. It would stop

the envoy of envelopes

from encouraging trips to the bank,

while catalyzing the repossessors—

who, unlike you, can have your stuff

without paying for it—

but a play cannot occur within another

without a similar comingling of rehearsals.

Behind the scenes *behind* the scenes,

since the initial meeting of final
cast and crew, everyone
has been hooking up, heading to their respective
post-work dives to complain about how
how much fun they're having has so little to do
with the divisibility of dollars into drinks,
pitting indulgence and the power to indulge
in opposition, on an x- and y-axis, respectively.

They do meet at a point, don't they?
So it's called zero-zero, so what?
The paint on the pavement could've made it
into a museum, but it was loaded onto the wrong truck.
Soft-handed restorers would guarantee
perpetual glimmer, so every generation could pretend
it's brand-new, but instead this white crosswalk—
a stack of skinny Rothkos—leads patrons to the theater,
shrouded in footsteps. Thus the perpendicularity
of the visual and dramatic arts (is drama visual art?)
expressed as a single actor crossing this street daily
dissolves into a field of isolated somnambulists,
so that realism burdens itself with confrontation
with the real, where a room of dreamers practices

"sound of snake hiss" by shaking maraca softly
from ear to ear of a microphone.

On closing night,
the director enters the play as The Director,
and the rolled newspaper he's pointing at the players
bears the headline, *Nobody's there.* (Is this enough
to break the frame, Joanna?) After the show,
warm food. Snow weighs down the theater, but it's spring
in every cast- and crewmember's mind: a line of prayer,
an address to a stranger, a force-from-beyond
who answers your insecurities with a grand
review of your performance, of all this time spent watching
the logic morph, the monsoon moving the moon.

Exit Audience. The play
as written and performed has ended,
but the second play, from the nucleus of the first,
disperses across the city as its hydra of plots
chainlinks under overpasses and up fire escapes,
some into bedrooms, some into ballrooms,
flung from heads and hands. No one talks
about the next century! It took us twenty to paint
a feeling, but it's not like the Old Masters

weren't making it up as well. It's enough
to keep you crushing your head under your pillow,
these thoughts, under the inertia of self-examination,
but eventually the sun stops waiting
for you to finish counting the steps.

Perplexed because nothing moves like us,
nothing thinks like us about whether a gigantic phantom
sculpted this world from dream-dew and molasses,
since no bird sees us and wishes they couldn't fly—
of course we want to watch *The Discobolus* hurl iron
across the amphitheater, that oculus upturned at the sky!
But this way we know more clearly his exertion.
The forest isn't a meadow of pianos in a painter's eye.
The sky auditions to play the sky inside, making these noises:

Sound of door opening.
Sound of door closing.
Sound of ominous organ music silencing knocks at the door.

Drama

After Mark Strand

I think of the redundant lives
Of people in dramas who know they'll die
And that they've been fired
In the real world, where it is our job
To watch them. The long walk home is the same
For us. One rose among a million bushes
Satisfies a city block. The blocks of sunset
Seen between buildings differ slightly,
As if the sky were a puzzle and the puzzle
A landscape in a different country, where their character
Pretended to be from and where someone else now
Watches them become a ghost. You could tell
By the cinematography when someone was standing
Behind them; when a car might cut into the screen
On one side and take a body with it through the other;
When the gun would be put away and a hand
Extended towards someone everyone watching
At home had been convinced to want shot.
However they go, they go home. Yellow paint
Chips off an old hospital trolley someone rides
One final time down the small hallway to the infinite,
As the split second of darkness between the commercial

For pills with various side effects and the moment
When the doctor in the real show walks in
Becomes what is behind the eyes, and that is peace.

A Conversation on Poetics

No the other one. Aristotle said

what? Surely we've evolved from there.

Surely story can be investigated

even proven false on false pretenses

even when the antidote is to marvel

as marbles marvel at the numb face

of thumbnail. It sounds better

than it is is a compliment. Since

when is musing better than music?

It's not like it doesn't come from us.

Intern of the Infinite

Nightmare, I am lost.
It is my job to say

nothing important. Everything
is backwards. No. Everything is

backwards backwards.
I don't know. I have these papers

and orthopedic sandals only.
Very little has survived

my mind, built up with bank
statements, statements

made point-blank
to the mirror, I

smile at the thought,
superior to many

a portrait? It is my job
to say something important

or be forgotten. When I run
out of things to say, I sing.

When I run out of songs
to sing, I run.

In Place of Heaven

Homer fuses the Fates in one,
but Hesiod says there's three:

One spins the thread, one divvies it up, one cuts it
with big scissors as if she were receiving a key
to the city. They watch us walk whatever street,
plotting our heartbeats according to unknown norms,
secret criteria. But where are the gods who'll finally tell us
what we've been feeling all along is the miracle they intended?

A bird smushed in the forest
reminds me of rolling pins. To hear,
right after, the sonic boom of many vultures' wings
flapping out of the trees high above us
and be startled by their number, and the force
they leave behind, shaking all the leaves, is to know
some freedom exists in solitary, sensual
pursuits not everyone can access,

and those who can, not too much. Maybe Homer
made them one because it took all three
to spin a life that gave time to solitary and sensual pursuits,
in addition to social obligations—not to mention art,
which, if you want real time for, requires some of it

to be sloshed out unto the world like red tide for many tourists
to come by and say, "This is not why

I came to the beach." Like my life, I wish this poem began
when I began to understand it. At first, I thought it was about
the quick confluence of contemporary and classic myth—
centaurs in car commercials, kings in their castles
with credit card debt—but this oracle already
was written into stone several centuries ago.

Many poems were harmed
in the making of this poem.
All of them mine.

Farewell to Poetry

for Shangyang Fang

I give myself to the end of this poem to decide.
I empty myself, have emptied myself 10,000 times,
like a lung. I guess that's a terrible estimate. We breathe a fuckton—
even when air has skunk taste and texture, as opposed
to its usual quiescence. Never thought I'd get to use
that word, quiescence, or specious, or obeisance, even though
I think a lot, which seems like a straight shot to writing,
yet side by side body and mind struggle to work in tandem,
but one at a time you feel the other melt into instinct,
yanking your hands out of the hearth or daydreaming about Kyoto
while a stranger who thinks you're staring at him makes a face
your eyes can't see, having flipped the iris inward
like a standing mirror before a bed a couple shamefully shares.
What makes us so deserving of space in other people's minds?
When the car window breaks open and you seal your blind spot
with a black garbage bag, as you're trying to change lanes,
do you remember how much we've complained about
ourselves, throwing meaning into our mischief like salt into a pool?
Beware! The sidewalk scorpions are prowling about the kitchen,
claws scraping through grout. Meanwhile we turn and turn,
first to some garden, briefly, next to a scatterbrained table,
before finally the shapeshifter's trench coat unhooks itself

from the shower rod. We take turns putting it on, choosing
the Invisibility setting, which we intuit as addictive
before retreating to our personas to deal with withdrawal.
Yet having developed a taste for breath we find we cannot stop
losing it. It's elusive as the glimmer of oil on asphalt, a blackbird's
coat bending to sunbeams. This is what we have decided to pursue,
bent on one leg, two ballerinas of imbalance. We are chasing it
up the parking garage, ignoring the various fonts
in which slurs are sharpied on stairwells before, on the roof,
we lose the color we sought in the light in a violent sunset,
yet go on staring into it, trying to read the negative language
the sun scribbles inside our eyelids. Yours says,
"Do not damage with your eye all that already shines."
Here's mine: "What are you staring at the sun for?
Some of its darkness it gets from us."

Notes

"Drum Solo" is written after Nicanor Parra's poem, "Piano Solo."

"Master of Fine Arts" is in conversation with Vicente Huidobro's famous line, *"El poeta es un pequeño Dios"* ("The poet is a little God").

"Stitches After Reading Márquez" was inspired by Gabriel García Márquez's masterwork, *100 Years of Solitude.*

The Milton quote in "Inferno Use Only" is from Book 5 of *Paradise Lost.*

"Up the Depths" borrows its title from the Tomas Tranströmer poem, "Schubertiana."

"Drama" is written after Mark Strand's poem, "Fiction."

The cover photo was taken on campus at the University of Denver during a walk that Ian Cappelli made me go on, even though I was tired.

Acknowledgments

To my family for their perpetual love and support. This book would never have been possible without you.

To my teachers and mentors for their guidance, wisdom, and encouragement now and over the years: Jane Miller, Dean Young, Tomás Q. Morín, Joanna Klink, Bret Anthony Johnston, Robert Hass, Roger Reeves, Lisa Olstein, Carrie Fountain, David Kirby, Barbara Hamby, Roberto Fernández, Erin Belieu, James Kimbrell, Andrew Epstein, Craig Filar, and Jenn Hilley.

To Shangyang Fang, Dustin Pearson, Johann Sarna, Rushi Vyas, Ian Cappelli, Suphil Lee Park, and Josh Stanek. Your care and attention to these poems and this book have been invaluable to me. To Nicolas Schutz, Jake Blumstein, Tepeu Potter, John Murray, Jackie Hare, Courtney Lewis, Tim Chalumeau, Brandon Galloway, Anthony Osei, Minghao Tu, Rachel Heng, Tracey Rose Peyton, Nandini Majumdar, Chidera Abii, and Vianey Soliz Hernández. Thank you for your love, time, and friendship.

To the Michener Center for Writers, Florida State University, the University of Denver, and the Fulbright Foundation for giving me the time and space to write and revise these poems.

To the editors of the following journals, where many of these poems first appeared, sometimes in different versions: *Bennington Review, The*

Cortland Review, Crazyhorse, Diode, Interim, Meridian, Missouri Review, New Delta Review, POETRY, Radar Poetry, River Styx, Sonora Review, The Shore, and *Tupelo Quarterly.*

And, finally, to Hannah Matheson, Ryan Murphy, Martha Rhodes, and everyone at Four Way Books: for your energy, your knowledge, and your belief in poetry—mine and otherwise.

About the Author

Daniel Ruiz is a Puerto Rican and Cuban poet and translator, a graduate of the Michener Center for Writers and Florida State University, and a two-time finalist for the National Poetry Series. In 2016, he was a Fulbright Scholar to Chile. Currently, he is pursuing a PhD in English & Literary Arts at the University of Denver, where he edits poetry and translations for the *Denver Quarterly*.

WE ARE ALSO GRATEFUL TO THOSE INDIVIDUALS WHO PARTICIPATED IN
OUR BUILD A BOOK PROGRAM. THEY ARE:

Anonymous (14), Robert Abrams, Debra Allbery, Nancy Allen,
Michael Ansara, Kathy Aponick, Jean Ball, Sally Ball, Jill Bialosky,
Sophie Cabot Black, Laurel Blossom, Tommye Blount, Karen and
David Blumenthal, Jonathan Blunk, Lee Briccetti, Jane Martha Brox,
Mary Lou Buschi, Anthony Cappo, Carla and Steven Carlson,
Robin Rosen Chang, Liza Charlesworth, Peter Coyote,
Elinor Cramer, Kwame Dawes, Michael Anna de Armas,
Brian Komei Dempster, Renko and Stuart Dempster,
Matthew DeNichilo, Rosalynde Vas Dias, Patrick Donnelly,
Charles R. Douthat, Lynn Emanuel, Blas Falconer, Laura Fjeld,
Carolyn Forché, Helen Fremont and Donna Thagard,
Debra Gitterman, Dorothy Tapper Goldman, Alison Granucci,
Elizabeth T. Gray Jr., Naomi Guttman and Jonathan Mead,
Jeffrey Harrison, KT Herr, Carlie Hoffman, Melissa Hotchkiss,
Thomas and Autumn Howard, Catherine Hoyser, Elizabeth Jackson,
Linda Susan Jackson, Jessica Jacobs, Deborah Jonas-Walsh,
Jennifer Just, Voki Kalfayan, Maeve Kinkead, Victoria Korth,
David Lee and Jamila Trindle, Rodney Terich Leonard,
Howard Levy, Owen Lewis and Susan Ennis, Eve Linn,
Matthew Lippman, Ralph and Mary Ann Lowen, Maja Lukic,
Neal Lulofs, Anthony Lyons, Ricardo Alberto Maldonado,
Trish Marshall, Donna Masini, Deborah McAlister, Carol Moldaw,
Michael and Nancy Murphy, Kimberly Nunes, Matthew Olzmann and
Vievee Francis, Veronica Patterson, Patrick Phillips, Robert Pinsky,
Megan Pinto, Kevin Prufer, Anna Duke Reach, Paula Rhodes,
Yoana Setzer, James Shalek, Soraya Shalforoosh, Peggy Shinner,
Joan Silber, Jane Simon, Debra Spark, Donna Spruijt-Metz,
Arlene Stang, Page Hill Starzinger, Catherine Stearns,
Yerra Sugarman, Arthur Sze, Laurence Tancredi, Marjorie and
Lew Tesser, Peter Turchi, Connie Voisine, Susan Walton,
Martha Webster and Robert Fuentes, Calvin Wei, Allison Benis White,
Lauren Yaffe, and Rolf Yngve.